The

Song of

A

Butterfly

A search for Love

By

Effie Darlene Barba

i

Published in Columbia Missouri by

Effie de Barba Publishing

P.O. Box 30829

Columbia, MO 65205-3829

(407) 506-5205

Case # 1-5260804141

Illustrations by:

Ronald Barba of

Ronin Ron's Custom Art

Cover Picture: Monarch

Photography of Sarah Barba

In Loving Memory of Pedro Barba, Jr.

(1/15/1942-7/23/1994)

And dedicated to my beautiful children Melissa (Moran) Smith, Alberto F. Barba, and Ronald B Barba who were always there for me.

The LORD is nigh unto them that are of a broken heart; and saveth such as be of a contrite spirit.

Psalm 34:18

For I am persuaded, that neither death, nor life, nor angels, nor principalities, nor powers, nor things present, nor things to come, Nor height, nor depth, nor any other creature, shall be able to separate us from the love of God, which is in Christ Jesus our Lord.

Romans 8:38-39

A little girl had called Your name

Began to feast upon Your word

And like a caterpillar came

To cherish comfort, truth was blurred

I thought that if I did what's right

You'd give me all my heart's delight

Had I forgotten it was Grace

That had saved a worm such as I

Within my heart pride took its place

Then I believed as truth the lie

That if You loved me as Your dear

You'd only fill my life with cheer

Above all else my one desire

To find the one who'd love me true

Enduring all I flamed that fire

And there He was, a gift from You

A human heart with broken soul

The pain of which did take its toll

Yet, willing heart my love stood firm

I bade you Lord to give me strength

Your love for me you did affirm

Unveiling all its depth and length

And then You took my earthly love

To be with you- Your home above

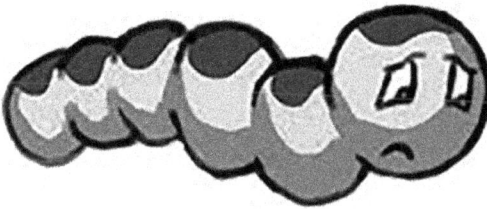

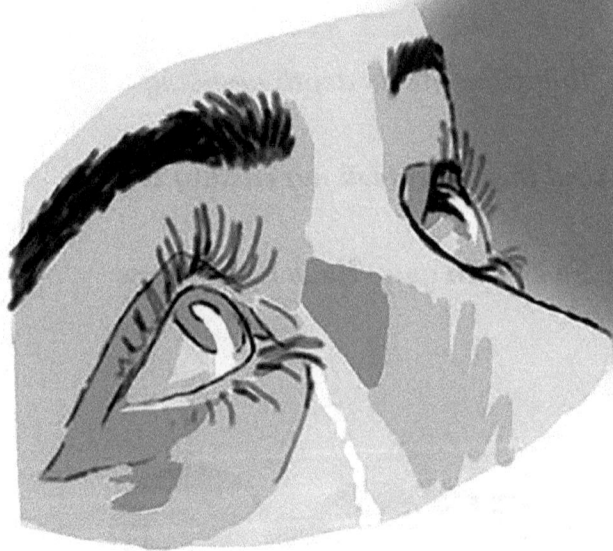

My sorrow came like bitter rain

I searched for love again to find

Attempts to love I did but feign

Until to loneliness resigned

I cannot tell you now the why

Despite Your love I still did cry

With Broken Heart-I drew within

And built a hard cocoon like shell

How was it that I thought therein?

I'd safe from pain and sorrow dwell

There within the dark cold wall

I heard God's voice, I heard You call

In darkness, there I felt Your Grace

I struggled, Lord your will to see

And there I saw Your love filled face

This gave me strength to then break free

So, there I'd sealed myself to die

And now emerged a butterfly

Oh wondrous Joy I know is mine

And Love abounding in this heart

Your Mercy, Grace and Glory Shine

Upon my life You did impart

The broken moments You did will

That I might fly above the hill

And now, Dear God; Your love in me

No longer wrought with fear or need

This heart of mine has been set free

To pour forth love in word and deed

To those I meet along this way

And fly with joy in You today.

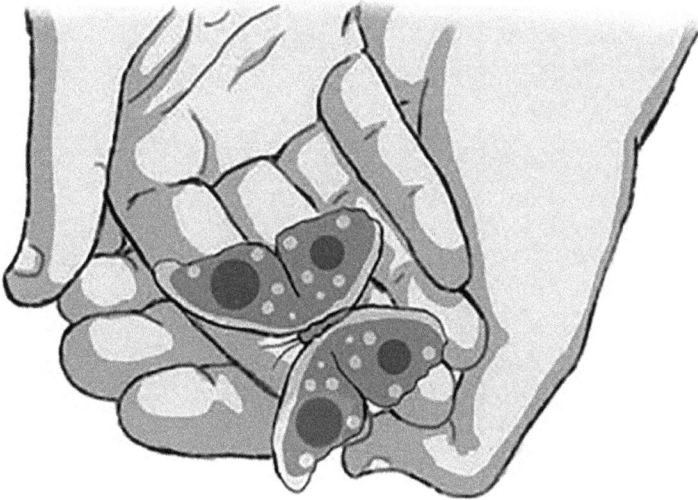

It took me a lifetime to discover the truth of love; but it has been worth every step of the journey; because of the joy I know now. Every tear, every heartbreak has lead me to today and I thank God that it did. Effie Darlene Barba

The Song of a Butterfly